STEROIDS

Erin Knight

Crabtree Publishing Company
www.crabtreebooks.com

Developed and produced by: Plan B Book Packagers
www.planbbookpackagers.com

Editorial director: Ellen Rodger

Art director: Rosie Gowsell-Pattison

Editor: Molly Aloian

Proofreader: Crystal Sikkens

Cover design: Margaret Amy Salter

Project coordinator: Kathy Middleton

**Production coordinator and
   prepress technician:** Katherine Berti

Print coordinator: Katherine Berti

Photographs:
Front cover: Yavuz Arslan/Das Fotoarchiv/
Photolibrary; Title page: Alexander Trinitatov/
Shutterstock.com; p. 6: Laurin Rinder/
Shutterstock.com; p. 8: Ilya Andriyanov/
Shutterstock.com; p. 9: oliveromg/Shutterstock.com;
p. 10: (top) 18percentgrey/Shutterstock.com; p. 11:
Losevsky Pavel/Shutterstock.com; p. 12: J. McPhail/
Shutterstock.com; p. 14: Bonita R. Cheshier/
Shutterstock.com; p. 17: Allen Berezovsky/
Shutterstock.com; p. 19: Pierre E. Debbas/
Shutterstock.com; p. 20: Jim Chernishenko;
p. 21: Rob Byron/Shutterstock.com; p. 22: Istvan
Csak/Shutterstock.com; p. 23: Coste Vlad Ionut/
Shutterstock.com; p. 24: Lasse Kristensen/
Shutterstock.com; p. 25: Ustin/Shutterstock.com;
p. 26: Dmitry Lobanov/Shutterstock.com; p. 28:
Chantal de Bruijne/Shutterstock.com; p. 30:
Cheryl Ann Quigley/Shutterstock.com; p. 32:
Darren Hubley/Shutterstock.com; p. 35: Istvan
Csak/Shutterstock.com; p. 36: bikeriderlondon/
Shutterstock.com; p. 37: Vlue/Shutterstock.com; p. 38:
Wave Break Media Ltd/Shutterstock.com; p. 41: William

Library and Archives Canada Cataloguing in Publication

Knight, Erin, 1980-
   Steroids / Erin Knight.

(Dealing with drugs)
Includes index.
Issued also in electronic format.
ISBN 978-0-7787-5511-1 (bound).--ISBN 978-0-7787-5518-0 (pbk.).

   1. Steroid abuse--Juvenile literature. I. Title. II. Series: Dealing
with drugs series

HV5822.S68K65 2011   j362.29'9   C2011-902562-0

Library of Congress Cataloging-in-Publication Data

Knight, Erin, 1980-
   Steroids / Erin Knight.
      p. cm. -- (Dealing with drugs)
   Includes index.
   ISBN 978-0-7787-5511-1 (reinforced library binding : alk. paper)
-- ISBN 978-0-7787-5518-0 (pbk. : alk. paper) -- ISBN 978-1-4271-
9729-0 (electronic pdf)
   1. Steroid abuse--Juvenile literature. I. Title. II. Series.

   HV5822.S68K65 2012
   613.8--dc22
                                                        2011013877

Crabtree Publishing Company

www.crabtreebooks.com   1-800-387-7650

Printed in the U.S.A./112011/JA20111018

Published in Canada
Crabtree Publishing
616 Welland Ave.
St. Catharines, Ontario
L2M 5V6

Published in the United States
Crabtree Publishing
PMB 59051
350 Fifth Avenue, 59th Floor
New York, New York 10118

Published in the United Kingdom
Crabtree Publishing
Maritime House
Basin Road North, Hove
BN41 1WR

Published in Australia
Crabtree Publishing
3 Charles Street
Coburg North
VIC 3058

Facts & Stats

- About one third of high school students who use steroids take them to improve their looks, not their athletic skills.

- When 198 Olympic hopefuls were asked the question, "If you knew that taking a banned substance would go undetected and guarantee you an Olympic medal, would you take it?" 195 said "yes."

- An estimated one to three million U.S. athletes abuse steroids.

- Surveys suggest that between four and eleven percent of high school boys have taken steroids, and that up to three percent of high school girls have tried them.

- Possession of anabolic steroids is punishable by one year in prison and a minimum $1,000 fine.

Introduction
Muscle and Myth

Have you ever wanted something so badly that you would do whatever it took to get it? What if somebody told you that a position on your school's varsity team or a college sports scholarship could be yours if only you were a little bit bigger or a few seconds faster? All you have to do to get there is take a few pills, or inject a few needles, and work out harder than ever before. Maybe you even know someone who is taking steroids, supplements, or **growth hormones**, and maybe you've seen the difference that these substances can make. So what's the catch? That's what this book will help you figure out.

Every year, the dream of being the next big sports star drives young athletes to put their bodies at risk and damage their future in the sport that they love. There are many different kinds of **performance-enhancing** drugs available to athletes of all ages. Anabolic steroids and prosteroids, human growth hormone, and **amphetamines** are just a few. Unfortunately, the list of harmful side effects is almost as long. Hair loss, acne, shriveled testicles, and breast growth in males, and facial hair and a deepening voice in females, are only the tip of the iceberg in terms of consequences.

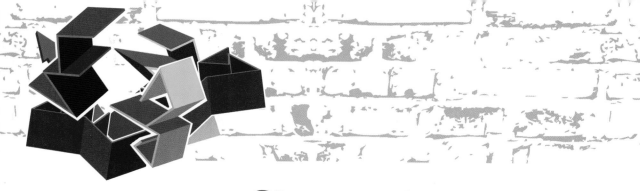

Chapter 1
What's the Big Deal?

Steroids fall into the category of ergogenic drugs. A drug that is classified as ergogenic is a substance that can be used to improve athletic performance. Other ergogenic drugs include **prohormones**, such as **androstenedione** and androstenediol, growth hormones, and **nutritional supplements**. While these substances may act on the body in different ways, the goals are the same: to gain muscle, increase **endurance**, and speed muscle and strength recovery.

Steroids, the most common performance-enhancing drugs, are a kind of hormone. Hormones are produced naturally by the body. The best known steroid hormone is testosterone, which is produced in greater quantities in men, and gives them male characteristics such as a deep voice and facial or body hair. Estrogen, a hormone produced by the female body, is also a steroid. Women produce some testosterone as well, but only about one tenth of what men produce. Many performance-enhancing steroids are designed to **mimic** testosterone, since this is the hormone that encourages muscle development.

Anabolic and Androgenic

Technically, steroids are known as anabolic androgenic steroids, because they have two kinds of effects: anabolic (muscle-building) effects, and androgenic (masculinizing) effects.

Legit Uses

When they were first **isolated**, steroids were thought to delay the effects of old age. While we now know this to be untrue, anabolic steroids can be very effective in certain medical treatments. Anabolic steroids are legally prescribed by doctors and used for people who have hormone deficiencies that prevent them from experiencing normal puberty. These drugs are also prescribed to burn victims to generate skin growth, to people recovering from surgeries, and to some cancer patients. Still, the number of people who use anabolic steroids illegally in order to gain a competitive edge is much greater than the number who are prescribed them for the treatment of health problems. Doctors never prescribe anabolic steroids for building muscle.

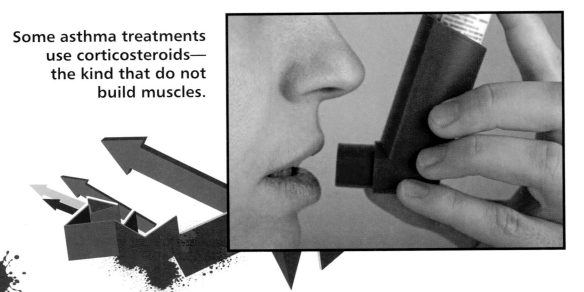

Some asthma treatments use corticosteroids— the kind that do not build muscles.

Teenagers are at the peak age for the natural production of hormones that build muscles.

Other Performance Enhancers

Athletes looking to build muscle will sometimes turn to drugs other than steroids. There are many reasons for this choice. Some people believe taking a nutritional supplement or a prohormone is not as risky as taking steroids. They think that if a product can be legally purchased over-the-counter, it can't be bad for them. Often, their decision to use other performance enhancers lies in their fear of getting caught. Some athletes choose to take human growth hormone (hGH) because they think it will be more difficult to detect if they are tested for steroid use.

Unfortunately, these beliefs are misleading. Alternatives to steroids can have just as many negative side effects, and the body-building benefits are not guaranteed. Studies show that high school athletes who used creatine—a compound said to help build muscles—gained no more muscle than they would have without the supplement. Many did however, experience some unpleasant side effects, such as muscle cramps, dizziness, and diarrhea.

Risky Venture

Taking any form of performance-enhancing drug comes with serious risk. There is risk to your health, risk to your reputation, and risk to your future in the sport. According to drug-regulation agencies, an athlete is responsible for whatever is in his or her body, so it is important to know how any substance you consume can affect you.

Athletes have been disciplined for testing positive for drugs that they claim they were unaware of taking. Romanian gymnast Andreea Raducan was stripped of her gold medal at the 2000 Sydney Olympics because her over-the-counter cold medication contained the banned substance pseudoephedrine.

Where Do You Find Them?

Some athletes and teens are able to convince their doctors that they require an ergogenic drug for a medical reason and get what in slang terms is called a "pass," or prescription. Others are given these drugs by coaches or trainers who have a lot invested in the success of their athletes. It is illegal for a coach or trainer to give any kind of drug to an athlete.

'Roid Slang

Illegal steroids used for bulking up are often called "gear" in the gym and on the street.

Preferred Supplier

Performance-enhancing drugs produced by **pharmaceutical** companies and sold by prescription through pharmacies are preferred by users because their production is regulated. In other words, the user knows exactly what drug he or she is taking and the exact dosage. Of course, not everyone has access to these legally produced drugs. Those who do not, turn to the **black market**, or underground economy, for their "gear."

The Athlete's Black Market

The illegal drug trade is a massive underground economy with ties throughout the world. Performance-enhancing drugs have been linked to organized crime in the U.S., Mexico, Russia, China, and other countries. These illegally produced drugs are often pushed on the street or at gyms, where dealers know they will find willing buyers. Unfortunately for the athlete, the people involved in the black market do not care about the serious health effects that their drugs might have.

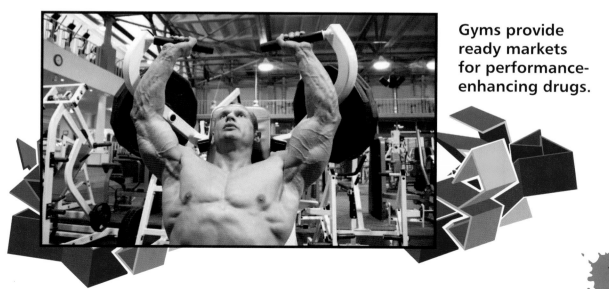

Gyms provide ready markets for performance-enhancing drugs.

What's In This Stuff?

Many of the performance-enhancing drugs bought on the black market contain impurities and are made with different ingredients than they claim. Some are complete fakes and contain no anabolic steroids. Others contain doses that are much higher than even an experienced steroid user would desire. Instead of these facts leading to more cautious use, an athlete might be so desperate to succeed that he or she will consume high quantities of several different black-market steroids, just to hedge their bets.

'Roids on the Web

These days, it is easy to find websites that sell performance-enhancing drugs online. A simple web search will turn up dozens of hits for retailers of nutritional supplements, prohormones, and steroids. Many are targeted specifically to teens, with catchy names that use terms such as "ripped" and "atomic" to suggest easy muscle gain. Some websites claim product **legitimacy** by suggesting they are overseen by medical doctors or experts in sports nutrition, in order to convince buyers of their product's safety and success rates.

Websites often try to convince readers that performance-enhancing substances are harmless.

The ideal body

With all of the dangers associated with performance-enhancing drugs, why do so many athletes and young people take the risk? The truth is, there is no simple answer. The high expectations placed on athletes by themselves, their families, their coaches, and their fans, can add pressure that is difficult for anyone to deal with. Whether a teen is looking to get a sports scholarship, a position on a school team, or just to look ripped, there is no shortage of role models and professional athletes who have shown that the way to succeed is to juice up. Former Major League Baseball players Jose Canseco and Jason Giambi, and Olympic champion Marion Jones are just a few of the high-profile athletes who admitted to taking performance-enhancing drugs. Many others have been accused, but refuse to admit use. It is hard for young people to say no thanks when they see the success of those using drugs.

Not Just Athletes

Young athletes are not the only ones affected by society's expectations. Many teens are worried that their bodies will never look like those of the models and movie stars who stare back from magazine covers. In fact, in a survey of boys ages 11 to 17, over half of them identified the "ideal body" with a **physique** that is so muscle-bound it could only be had by using steroids. Society idealizes muscular good looks, so it should not be surprising that one-third of all high school steroid users are taking the drugs to look better and not to improve their athletic skill.

Chapter 2
Blame the Game?

Synthetic testosterone had not been available for very long before athletes were tempted to use it to gain an advantage in their sport. In the 1950s, competitive bodybuilders began experimenting with testosterone **injections**. These athletes found that the male hormone helped them gain the muscle mass and definition they needed to win over the competition judges.

Heavy Lifting

Weightlifting is a sport with a long history of doping, or using performance-enhancing drugs. The U.S. weightlifting team was no match for the Russians at the 1952 Olympic Games in Helsinki, Finland. That year the Russian team won medals in seven events. Dr. John Ziegler, the U.S. team's doctor, later discovered that the Russian training program included regular use of testosterone. Not wanting to be out-matched by their rivals, he helped develop the steroid Dianabol for his athletes. Dianabol is still used today. Athletes in other events slowly began to give in to the temptation of performance-enhancing drugs. Today, it is difficult to find a sport that does not have some record of drug abuse.

A Necessary Evil?

Although Dr. Ziegler, sometimes called the "Father of Anabolics," was pleased with the results of his experiments, he died wishing he had never been involved with the drugs. At the time, he believed that doping was the only way for his team to win the gold medal back from the Russians. This attitude is still reflected in the decisions of many athletes and coaches to use performance-enhancing drugs. Many believe that if everybody else is doing it, then not only is it okay for them to do it too, but that they have to take the drugs if they are going to compete successfully. There is even a term for clean athletes who are affected psychologically by knowing many of their rivals are using performance enhancers: passive doping.

A Disadvantage?

Athletes at both the college and professional level have come forward to suggest that the use of performance-enhancing drugs is more rampant than you might have guessed. The fact that playing clean is sometimes called playing naked, suggests that an athlete who does not depend on drugs for his or her performance will be at a disadvantage to those who do.

Natural Reaction

Some athletes take the herb ephedra, also known as ma huang. Although natural, ephedra can cause reactions such as seizures, increased heart rate, insomnia, and paranoia. The death of Baltimore Orioles pitcher Steven Bechler in 2003 is believed to have been caused by ephedra.

What if Our Heroes Do It?

Knowing that some of your teammates might be doping—and feeling like you need to, too, if you want to keep up—is one of the many reasons young people feel that taking performance-enhancing drugs is worth the risk. Sports heroes play a huge role in our society today. Pro sports stars, world champions, and Olympic gold medalists receive hefty paychecks and celebrity status. Those who never get called up from the minors or finish fourth at the Olympics are quickly forgotten. How does this affect the young athletes who have followed the careers of their heroes since they were young?

Although the doping allegations and admissions by major athletes may lose the athletes some fans, others get the impression that using performance-enhancing drugs is the only way to have a chance at big time success.

Professional athletes are treated like celebrities. They attend red carpet events and are paid a lot of money to endorse products. The popularity can be intoxicating.

Taylor Hooton's Story

Taylor Hooton was a 16-year-old baseball pitcher with a dream of making the big leagues. Baseball was in his blood. His cousin, Burt Hooton, had been a starting pitcher for the Chicago Cubs, and Taylor himself was one of the best on his team.

He had everything going for him. Then his high school coach told him he needed to be bigger. Taylor had always worked hard. How was he supposed to bulk up without doing something differently? He knew that others on his team were already on 'roids, so he figured that he should give it a try.

Sure, he got bigger. He gained 30 pounds of muscle within a few months, but he also experienced severe acne, bad breath, cramps, and violent mood swings.

His family was worried by the changes they saw, but it was a while before they began to suspect that Taylor was on steroids. Like so many others, his parents thought their son could handle the pressure that came with his talent.

It all came to an end on July 15, 2003. After a bout of depression and a serious argument with his family, Taylor Hooton hung himself in his bedroom.

His parents established the Taylor Hooton Foundation in his memory. The foundation's goal is to educate youth about the dangers of anabolic steroids and appearance- and performance-enhancing drugs. Their website, taylorhooton.org, has useful information about steroids, chat sessions with athletic trainers, and details about how to schedule a speaking engagement at your school.

Pressure to Be the Best

Though watching pro sports has long been one of America's favorite pastimes, college-level sports are also very popular. Games are often televised and played in a stadium filled with up to 100,000 screaming fans. With extra exposure for college athletes comes extra pressure to be a star. High school students hope to be scouted for a spot on the varsity team or to secure a sports scholarship which might be the only way they can afford college tuition. It might be hard to turn down the first person who offers you something that will give your body a boost, especially if you think you are a little bit smaller than some of your teammates. But these drugs come with a cost, and are more dangerous to take the younger you are.

It can be thrilling having so many people, parents, and strangers alike, cheering for your team. Sports stars are put on a pedestal and often given perks for performance. That creates a lot of pressure to do well.

Gateway Substances?

In the U.S., anabolic steroids are classified as a Schedule III Controlled Substance. This means that they have a significant potential for abuse and are illegal without a doctor's prescription. Some adolescent and teen players are not comfortable getting into illegal drugs right away. Some try out supplements, such as creatine or prohormones, first, thinking that these legal performance enhancers will give them the edge they need without having to turn to the hard stuff. Some products are marketed specifically to younger consumers, although the American College of Sports Medicine says that many of these products are not recommended for youths under the age of 18.

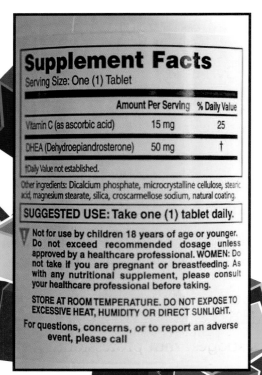

Supplement Facts
Serving Size: One (1) Tablet

	Amount Per Serving	% Daily Value
Vitamin C (as ascorbic acid)	15 mg	25
DHEA (Dehydroepiandrosterone)	50 mg	†

†Daily Value not established.

Other ingredients: Dicalcium phosphate, microcrystalline cellulose, stearic acid, magnesium stearate, silica, croscarmellose sodium, natural coating.

SUGGESTED USE: Take one (1) tablet daily.

Not for use by children 18 years of age or younger. Do not exceed recommended dosage unless approved by a healthcare professional. WOMEN: Do not take if you are pregnant or breastfeeding. As with any nutritional supplement, please consult your healthcare professional before taking.

STORE AT ROOM TEMPERATURE. DO NOT EXPOSE TO EXCESSIVE HEAT, HUMIDITY OR DIRECT SUNLIGHT.

For questions, concerns, or to report an adverse event, please call

Taking nutritional supplements is costly, and an athlete may not see the same results as a teammate who is on anabolic steroids or other illegal performance-enhancing drugs. An athlete may feel tempted to move on to the illegal and more dangerous drugs.

Bottle instructions on legal prohormones often warn against taking them before you are 18. This is because they can interfere with your body's natural ability to make hormones.

Prosteroids and Sports

Prosteroids, also known as prohormones or steroid precursors, are natural hormones that are converted to testosterone after they have been ingested. A related supplement, dehydroepiandrosterone (DHEA) can be legally purchased but is banned by the National Collegiate Athletic Association (NCAA) and some other sports associations.

Prosteroids are not proven to give significant athletic advantage. In fact, they initially stimulate testosterone production, but their use also leads to increases in estrogen production, which can lead to the development of breasts in males (known as gynecomastia). The popularity of prosteroids sharply increased after Major League Baseball (MLB) hero Mark McGwire admitted to using androstenedione, a naturally-occurring steroid available in dietary supplements. McGwire didn't confess to taking anabolic steroids until early 2010, but could freely admit to using prohormones back in 1998, because they were not on the list of MLB's banned substances. Even now, the regulations for professional sports leagues are weaker than they are for amateur sports competitions such as the Olympics. The penalties for an Olympic athlete who tests positive are far greater than for a professional athlete. As a result, MLB, the National Football League (NFL), and the National Hockey League (NHL), have all been criticized. Critics suggest that professional leagues care more about profit than about keeping their sport clean.

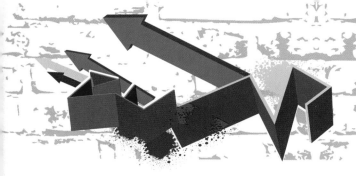

Chapter 3
Your Body on 'Roids

An athlete who takes performance-enhancing drugs is doing it with a specific goal in mind. This goal depends on the sport. An endurance athlete may want a lean body that can train hard and recover quickly, while a weightlifter or football player wants to be beefy and muscular. Athletes will take different combinations of drugs that they believe will give them the desired effect. The kinds of drugs they take also depend on where they are in their training. They may be aiming for "bulking," "cutting," "muscle-hardness," or simply "maintenance."

Athletes who are doping rarely take only one kind of drug. More commonly, they will do what is called stacking, which means combining a number of drugs in order to have the best chance at success. Unfortunately, stacking can also lead to overdose and greater chances of permanently damaging vital organs.

Many steroids are injected, which means the dose has to be precise and injected properly.

How Steroids Work

Whether steroids are taken orally, as an injection, as a cream, or through a skin patch, they all work in the body the same way. The steroid travels through the body and binds to the testosterone receptor in the muscle cell. Once the testosterone binds to the cell, the cell is stimulated to produce more protein, which is needed for muscle development.

Testosterone is the main ingredient of any anabolic steroid. It does not matter if testosterone is synthetically or naturally produced. The body will use it in the same way. Synthetic testosterone has the same molecular structure as natural testosterone. In addition to producing new muscle cells, testosterone also has an anti-catabolic effect. This means that it prevents the loss of muscle that comes with overuse, fatigue, or simply through the natural life-cycle of a cell. Steroid users will see fast results because their muscles can recover quickly from even the most intense workout. Of course, the drug doesn't do all the work. Users also need to train heavily and eat a diet high in protein.

Pyramid Builders

Steroid users usually take their drugs in cycles of four to twelve weeks. They will begin with a smaller dose that is gradually increased throughout the cycle, and then they will take a break from that particular drug. This process is called pyramiding.

The Big, the Bad, and the Ugly

Nothing comes without a cost. Steroids affect the body's organs and sexual functions, and the user's mind and behavior. Some of the first side effects users will notice are bad breath, skin rashes, and severe acne. Steroids also affect the brain's limbic system, which is the system responsible for mood, learning, and memory. You've probably heard the term "'roid rage." High levels of testosterone at work in the bodies of steroid users can cause mood swings and loss of control. It can be difficult to concentrate and reason with yourself. Many of the teen suicides that have been related to steroid use were probably a result of the crushing depression caused by hormonal fluctuations.

In one survey of steroid users, 77 percent reported suffering from one or more side effects, including shrunken testicles, development of breast tissue, high blood pressure, and disease.

Wacky Hormones

When the body is blindsided by huge amounts of a hormone, its natural cycles and functions are thrown off. It stops producing its own testosterone because it already has a surplus. It will try to filter the substance through the liver. People who use steroids over the long-term will often suffer from liver problems such as cysts or bleeding in the liver.

Effects on the teenage body

Adolescents and teens are at the greatest risk for long-term side effects from performance-enhancing drugs. Young bodies are naturally in a state of rapid development. The kind of hormone imbalance that results from steroid use can cause permanent harm by slowing and even stunting growth.

Some bodybuilders think they are going "natural" by using insulin, a hormone that regulates glucose in the blood and can help them build muscle. Diabetics use insulin to control their disease. Insulin is sometimes used to build stamina and muscles because it is undetectable. Too much insulin causes low blood sugar and can lead to a coma.

Ergogenic drug	Health effects
Anabolic steroids	• Organ damage (liver, heart, circulatory system) • Severe skin conditions • Testicular atrophy, reduced sperm count, breast development (males) • Deepened voice, facial & body hair growth, enlarged clitoris, menstrual disruption • Aggression & depression
Prohormones (androstenedione)	• Increased estrogen in men • Other effects similar to anabolic steroid use
DHEA	• Increased estrogen in men • Unsafe impurities
Growth hormone	• Bone fusion leading to stunted growth in teens
Creatine	• Dehydration • Muscle cramps • Digestive problems • Reduced kidney function
Ephedra alkalies	• Heart attack & stroke • Seizures • Psychosis • High blood pressure • Death

Chapter 4
Steroid History

For as long as there have been sports competitions, athletes have tried to find a winning potion—something they can take that will perfectly prepare their bodies and give them an advantage over their opponents. The ancient Greeks prepared for the Olympics by drinking concoctions of wine, the poison strychnine, and **hallucinogenic** mushrooms, and by eating sesame seeds to increase their endurance.

In the 1800s, athletes would stimulate their bodies by taking caffeine, cocaine, strychnine, opium, and heroin. Cyclists in the early days of the Tour de France cycling race took combinations of drugs such as strychnine, chloroform, and cocaine to give themselves energy and deaden the pain of the long race. Amphetamines, also known as uppers, became popular with baseball players and other athletes in the '50s. There were no regulations against doping at that time and most athletes did not consider taking these substances to be cheating. They thought of them as necessary, although dangerous, measures to gain an advantage and be number one in their sport.

'Roid Research

Natural testosterone was difficult to obtain, but physicians knew that it was an important hormone with great medical potential. The 1939 **Nobel Prize** for Chemistry was awarded to researchers Leopold Ruzicka and Adolf Butenandt, who had figured out how to make a synthetic testosterone. The synthetic compound has since been manipulated to create over 100 different kinds of anabolic androgenic steroids.

Help the Wounded

During World War II, steroids were used to treat wounded soldiers, to help patients recover from surgery, and even in an attempt to bring survivors of concentration camps back from the brink of starvation. It didn't take long before people realized steroids might be used to gain an advantage in competition. The first reported use of steroids in sports was on a racing horse, Holliday, in 1941. Racetracks now closely regulate against the doping of horses, as steroids have the same ergogenic effects on animals as they do on humans.

Horse racing is a sport that monitors and tests for doping.

Discouraging the Dopers

Performance enhancers have been used in amateur and professional sports for a long time. Drug testing in competition is fairly new by comparison. The first Olympic drug tests were introduced at the 1968 Olympic Games when doping threatened to tarnish the reputation of the Games. The World Anti-Doping Agency (WADA), a neutral third-party agency that tests amateur Olympic-level athletes, wasn't set up until 1999. Professional sports leagues have less strict testing requirements and often fairly lenient punishments for dopers.

One of the difficulties in discouraging drug use is that because the stakes are so high, all parties involved stand to gain big. However, some can also lose big. In Olympic competition, it is in a country's interest to produce winners. Athletes caught doping can lose their medals and be banned from competition. In professional sports, athletes who win are rewarded with higher salaries. Winning teams sell more tickets. Until recently, doping was often accepted or ignored in many professional sports. The NFL, NHL, and MLB all have drug testing policies that were developed after players were caught or admitted to taking performance-enhancing drugs. Players are now randomly tested for steroids and other substances. Punishments for use range from suspensions to fines.

Chapter 5
Dependence and Addiction

Drug dependence happens because the body will always try to adapt to the substances we consume. A person with **chronic** pain, for instance, will require higher doses of pain medication as the body builds a greater **tolerance**. Although steroids are not as physically addictive as some drugs, they do alter the body's natural hormone production. The body recognizes that it has too much testosterone and reacts by shutting down further production. When testosterone levels drop, the athlete will experience mood swings and begin to lose the muscle mass that he or she worked so hard to get.

Most steroid users begin to take the drugs because they want to be bigger, stronger, and faster. Once they see results, they fear that if they go off the drug they will become weak. This psychological dependence can be even more powerful than a physical dependence. There is even a term for it: muscle dysmorphia. A person suffering from muscle dysmorphia will look in the mirror and see a weakling. No matter how big he or she gets, it is still not big enough.

Dependence and Mood Disturbances

Psychological dependence on steroids is often evident in the violent mood swings and personality changes experienced by users. One study suggests that 23 percent of steroid users suffer from serious emotional distress, such as mania and severe depression. Users will often swing between feeling **euphoric** and invincible to feeling reckless, irritable, or enraged. Former NFL star Lyle Alzado was nicknamed rainbow because of his unpredictable moods. He described the emotional rush of using steroids as mentally addicting. His steroid use is believed to be behind his violent behaviors and his early death from cancer at age 43.

Behavioral Signs

The Diagnostic and Statistic Manual of Mental Disorders (DSM) has a set of criteria for determining substance dependence and abuse. Using these criteria, about 50 percent of all steroid users act in ways that suggest dependence. These actions include: developing tolerance, experiencing withdrawal symptoms, using higher doses than intended, being unable to cut down, and using the drug despite negative effect.

Everybody Is An Expert

The Internet is a confusing and often dangerous source for information on bodybuilding. Some sites give useful information such as how to maintain a proper diet for bodybuilding. Others promote the use of steroids and hormones. It can be hard to know what to trust.

Risk Leads to Risk

Teens who are dependent on steroids are more likely to put themselves at risk in other ways, as well. The mood swings and feelings of invincibility often cause young athletes to engage in other risk-taking activities that they might normally avoid. These social risks range from fighting, driving drunk and having unsafe sex, to experimenting with other drugs.

Injecting steroids is also a high-risk activity. You might think that everybody knows to avoid using dirty needles, but if your teammates are passing around the juice, it might not seem like a big deal. In fact, 25 to 33 percent of teen steroid users admit to sharing needles. This puts teens in danger of contracting incurable diseases such as HIV and hepatitis. Most users of performance-enhancing drugs rely on dealers for their "gear." Subjecting yourself to the black market is a dangerous activity in itself.

Steroids bought on the street or behind closed doors at the gym can be either completely useless or highly concentrated, and they often have harmful impurities. The trouble is, you often won't find out until it is too late.

Steroid use can lead to other risky behaviors.

35

How Bad Can it Be?

Once a person has committed to doing whatever it takes to look or perform his or her best, it is common to try to rationalize the decision. Teens might feel like they are too young to be in any serious danger from steroid use. They may believe that their bodies will bounce back or that the consequences they have heard about will only happen to other people. If a coach or an older player you respect tells you that steroids are no big deal, it might be easier to believe that person instead of answering the difficult questions you might have yourself.

Actually, young people are not the only ones to underestimate the dangers of steroids. For years, medical experts disagreed about the performance benefits of steroids. As a result, users thought that if doctors could be wrong about that, they might be wrong about their health warnings, too.

Our knowledge of what is a good diet and proper training for athletes has changed over the years.

Where's the Proof?

One of the difficulties with demonstrating the medical risks associated with steroid use, especially in teens, is that there are ethical problems with conducting potentially dangerous experiments on human subjects. For example, the violent behavior often termed "'roid rage" is most often seen in users who take around 1000 mg of the drug a week. While this is not uncommon in steroid users, participants in a study would never be prescribed such a high amount.

No matter what sorts of pressures you feel to be your best, try to remember that the medical problems associated with steroid use are greater than any performance benefits you might experience.

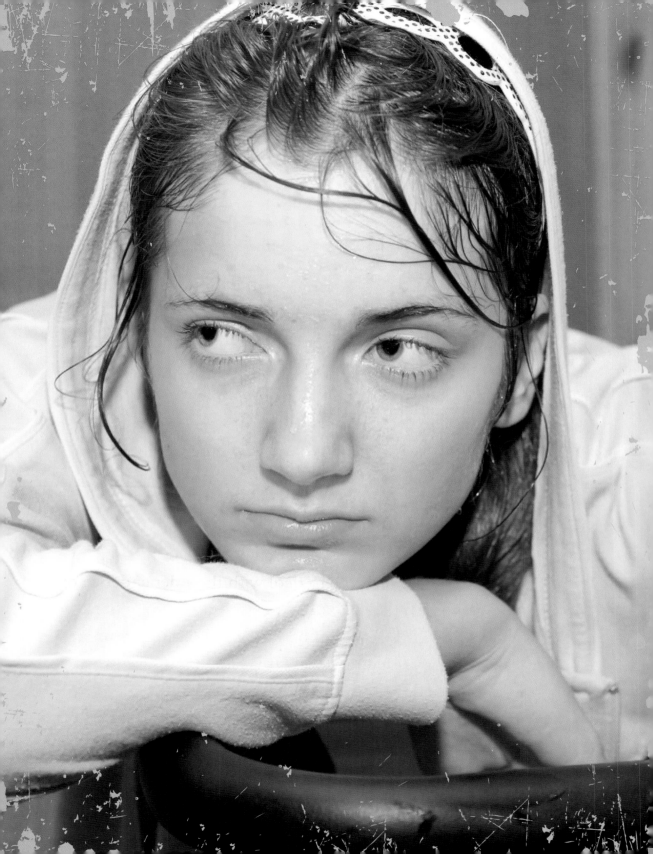

Chapter 6
Seeking Help

Once you know the facts about steroids, you are in a better position to identify when you or somebody you know might need to find help. If you recognize any of the behaviors associated with substance abuse, such as using higher and higher doses, feeling helpless about using the drugs, or skipping events or activities that you would normally attend, it might be time to talk to someone you trust.

Steroids are often believed to be less physically addicting than other street drugs, so there tends to be fewer treatment programs. In fact, many users will struggle to deal with their dependence or addiction on their own, thinking that they should be strong enough to kick it without help. Coming off performance-enhancing drugs can be incredibly hard. It is challenging physically, **psychologically**, and even socially. If you have been doping for a while, you likely have teammates or friends who are doing the same and who think that doing the drugs is no big deal.

Signs a Friend May Need Help

Sometimes it seems like we know our friends better than we know ourselves. Maybe you have noticed that a friend has been acting differently, and you suspect that performance-enhancing drugs might be the reason. If you notice any of the signs or behaviors in the list below, you may want to start thinking about what you can do to help.

Warning signs:
- trying to hide acne on the face and back
- looking bloated around the face or body
- bad breath
- rapid muscle growth, especially in the upper body
- trouble sleeping
- being preoccupied with winning
- showing irrational, reckless, or aggressive behavior

Try not to be too confrontational or accusatory when you approach a friend. He or she might immediately go on the defensive. Offer your support and make suggestions about who to contact for help, but remember that the decision to get clean has to be made by your friend.

Reaching Out

It might be easier to disclose your steroid use if you plan what you want to say ahead of time. If you really feel uncomfortable, try writing a letter to the person you have chosen to approach. Don't be afraid of telling the truth or talking about your feelings.

What Being Strong Really Means

Disclosure means to voluntarily reveal information about yourself. It is normal to feel vulnerable and scared when you decide to disclose to someone you trust that you have been using performance-enhancing drugs and you would like to stop. You might think that strength was something you get from pumping iron at the gym, but really being strong means that you are brave enough to talk about your steroid use. As you move through the steps to get clean, remember that you have proven how strong you are by taking responsibility for your problem and making the decision to get clean.

People Who Can Help

If you decide you need help, choose someone you trust and approach that person in a private place—somewhere you can feel as comfortable as possible. You might want to talk to your coach, your family doctor, the school counselor, a relative, or a friend. Even though you may have thought that your steroid use was your own dirty secret, the people closest to you may have already noticed changes in your appearance and behavior. The person you confide in will probably feel relieved that you have decided to seek help.

Just knowing that somebody else shares your secret can make the situation easier to handle.

Chapter 7
Treatment and Recovery

If you have committed to getting clean and playing true, you have already made the first important steps toward your goal. Maybe you have tried to kick your habit in the past and can recognize some of the symptoms and emotions that many people feel during treatment for their drug addiction.

Physical Symptoms

Users of performance-enhancing drugs do experience physical withdrawal symptoms. The most common symptoms are headaches, muscle aches, and joint pain. You may lose your appetite or experience digestive upset. It is not uncommon to feel dizzy as a result of the drop in blood pressure you will experience. You can expect to feel tired as your body tries to deal with the sudden drop in hormone levels. One of the most alarming physical signs of withdrawal for athletes is their rapid loss of muscle. Even if you keep working out, you will not be able to maintain the muscle mass that you gained while taking steroids or other performance-enhancing drugs. Try to remember that those muscles are the byproduct of the drug, not the sign of health and athleticism.

Mental symptoms

Mood swings and depression are very common during steroid withdrawal. We don't realize just how closely our moods are related to the hormone levels in our bodies. It will take a while for your body to learn how to stabilize its hormones again. It might help to talk to someone close to you about these emotions, or to keep a journal to record your moods and remind yourself that they are symptoms of withdrawal and not representations of your actual worth.

You may experience doubt and frustration and wonder why you decided to try to quit steroids in the first place. You might also feel isolated and cut off from your friends, especially if some of these friends are still taking steroids and are not supportive of your decision to get clean. The impact on your social life can be even more difficult to deal with than the physical discomfort you are experiencing. Sometimes these feelings of depression, frustration, and loneliness will get too strong for you to deal with on your own. It might be time to turn to one of the treatment options available in your community.

Treatment Options

No one will think less of you if you decide that you need help to beat your dependence. At different stages in your recovery, you will probably find yourself turning to friends, family, counselors, doctors, and coaches. These people will be your allies as you take back control of your life.

Therapy—Talking It Out

Some users find that supportive therapy is enough to help them deal with the physical, emotional, and social fallout of steroid recovery. The kind of therapy will depend on your individual needs, but it usually involves both one-on-one counseling and group sessions. It can be incredibly helpful to realize that other people have also made the decision to get clean and are experiencing similar challenges. Supportive therapy might also include alternative medical practices, such as acupuncture, massage, and meditation, which can be surprisingly effective in giving you the mental strength you need to meet your goal of getting clean.

If physical withdrawal symptoms become too severe, doctors can prescribe medication to help moderate them. Just as often, though, it is the emotional side effects that cause a user to be hospitalized. Severe depression or suicidal thoughts can very quickly become too big to deal with on your own. Even if medication or hospitalization is necessary, it is only one step in your treatment program. There will still be hard work that needs to be done as you move through the stages of recovery.

Resources

There are many sources offering information on performance-enhancing drugs. Some sources are more reliable than others. Look for books and websites that offer information and support for drug-free training, or ending dependency. Here are some trustworthy resources that can help you:

Books

Steroid Nation: Juiced Home Run Totals, Anti-aging Miracles, and a Hercules in Every High School: The Secret History of America's True Drug Addiction, by Shaun Assael (New York: Hyperion, 2007). This is a behind-the-scenes look at the popularity of steroids in America.

The Juice: The Real Story of Baseball's Drug Problems, by Will Carroll (Chicago: Ivan R. Dee, 2006). Sports columnist Will Carroll explains how steroids work and how they affect the body.

Websites:

www.justthinktwice.com/drugs/steroids.html
A site for teens with drug facts and fiction, personal stories, and advice. Find out real-life information about steroids and all kinds of drugs, or submit a question anonymously that will be answered by teens like you.

http://taylorhooton.org/
The official website of the Taylor Hooton Foundation has loads of information directed to young athletes and teens who might be tempted to turn to steroids.

www.steroidabuse.org/
This site is a great source of information about steroids and other drugs, addiction, and treatment. Click on NIDA for Teens-Anabolic steroids, a link about the science of drug abuse, for advice from your peers, treatment options, and free downloads.

Organizations

Narcotics Anonymous (www.na.org) will give you information about the support systems that are available in your community.

ATLAS (Athletes Training & Learning to Avoid Steroids, www.atlasprogram.com) and ATHENA (Athletes Targeting Healthy Exercise and Nutrition Alternatives, www.athenaprogram.com) are organizations that aim to educate young people about standing up to peer pressure, dealing with expectations, and finding alternatives to performance-enhancing drugs.

The National Collegiate Athletic Association (NCAA, www.ncaa.org) provides you with accurate information about your responsibilities as an athlete.

The United States Anti-Doping Agency (USADA, www.usantidoping.org) promotes clean competition through drug research, testing, and education programs.

The World Anti-Doping Agency (WADA, www.wada-ama.org/en/) is responsible for preventing drug use at the Olympics and other international events. They conduct drug-testing and determine the annual list of prohibited substances. Click "Youth Zone" on their website to make a commitment to being part of the "Play True Generation."

Glossary

amphetamines Addictive stimulant drugs that alter moods or are used with a prescription to help control some medical conditions

androstenedione A steroid hormone produced naturally by the human body and also manufactured as a dietary supplement. It is banned by the World Anti-Doping Agency and banned for sale in the U.S.

black market A term used to describe something sold illegally or "underground"

chronic Long lasting and difficult to change

endurance The ability to maintain strength or last longer in a task or sport

euphoric Feeling incredible or intense happiness or excitement

growth hormones Hormones that stimulate growth in humans, animals, and plants

hallucinogenic Something, such as a drug, that causes someone to hallucinate, or see or hear something that does not exist

injections Using a needle to inject, or put a drug directly into the bloodstream

isolated In science, to obtain an extract, or part of something such as a compound

legitimacy To make something seem right, acceptable, or normal

mimic To imitate or resemble

Nobel Prize An international prize awarded each year to researchers who do important work in many fields of science and medicine

nutritional supplements Preparations such as drinks, special food, or pills that claim to provide needed nutrients and vitamins for muscle growth

performance-enhancing Something such as a drug or a steroid that claims to make athletes build muscles and perform better

pharmaceutical Relating to medicinal drugs produced by drug companies

physique The form and size of a person's body

psychologically Something related to the mental state of a person

tolerance In drug use, tolerance means a user's body has gotten used to a drug or a certain dosage of a drug, and the body does not respond to it as well as it used to—often requiring more for the desired effect

Index